Mermaids

Concept and photographs by
BERNARD ROSA

Written by
JACKIE FRENCH

Angus&Robertson
An imprint of HarperCollins*Publishers*

Angus&Robertson
An imprint of HarperCollins*Publishers*, Australia

First published in Australia in 1995

Concept and photographs copyright © Bernard Rosa 1995
Text copyright © Jackie French 1995

This book is copyright.
Apart from any fair dealing for the purposes of private study, research, criticism or review,
as permitted under the Copyright Act, no part may be reproduced by any process without written permission.
Inquiries should be addressed to the publishers.

HarperCollins*Publishers*
25 Ryde Road, Pymble, Sydney, NSW 2073, Australia
31 View Road, Glenfield, Auckland 10, New Zealand
77–85 Fulham Palace Road, London W68JB, United Kingdom
Hazelton Lanes, 55 Avenue Road, Suite 2900, Toronto, Ontario M5R 3L2
and 1995 Markham Road, Scarborough, Ontario M1B 5M8, Canada
10 East 53rd Street, New York NY 10032, USA

National Library of Australia Cataloguing-in-Publication data:

Rosa, Bernard.
   Mermaids.

   ISBN 0 207 18919 6.
   1. Mermaids - Pictorial works - Juvenile literature.
   2. Mermaids - Juvenile literature. I. French, Jackie.
   II. Title.
   398.21

Printed in Hong Kong

9 8 7 6 5 4 3 2 1
99 98 97 96 95

*Dedicated to the dreams of children, that they may continue
to dream a perfect planet, where all creatures can live in harmony.
So be it — B.R.*

To Mandy who listens to mermaids — J.F.

Yesterday I dived with seagull wings;

the sea was a sharp white cloud that prickled on my skin.

Last week I climbed through bright green jungles in the waves.

Today I'll leap over the mountains

till they shudder and fall down.

Tomorrow I'll swim to the far horizon

and slip between the wrinkle at the edge of the sea and sky.

The Perfect Shell

You need to find the perfect shell,
one with an echo like an angry wave.
You need to find the perfect rock to sit on,
the perfect match of tide and moon and wind ...
And then you blow ...

The clouds rip apart,
the dolphins arch and dance.
And ships fly from their courses
pulled by your song.

And then you'll laugh
and swim away
while the shell drifts down through sunlit layers of water
and far off sailors whisper,
'You'll only hear a mermaid once in a lifetime
unless you answer her so she'll sing to you again.'

Seahorse

Once a sailor saw a child riding on a seahorse's back,
plunging through the crests of waves. 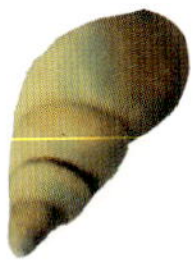
He shook his head and laughed. 
'I'm just imagining it,' he said.
But all that night he dreamed
of deep sea mountains weathered by the salt and tides,
of hidden pools beneath the deeper waters
where no sun shines.

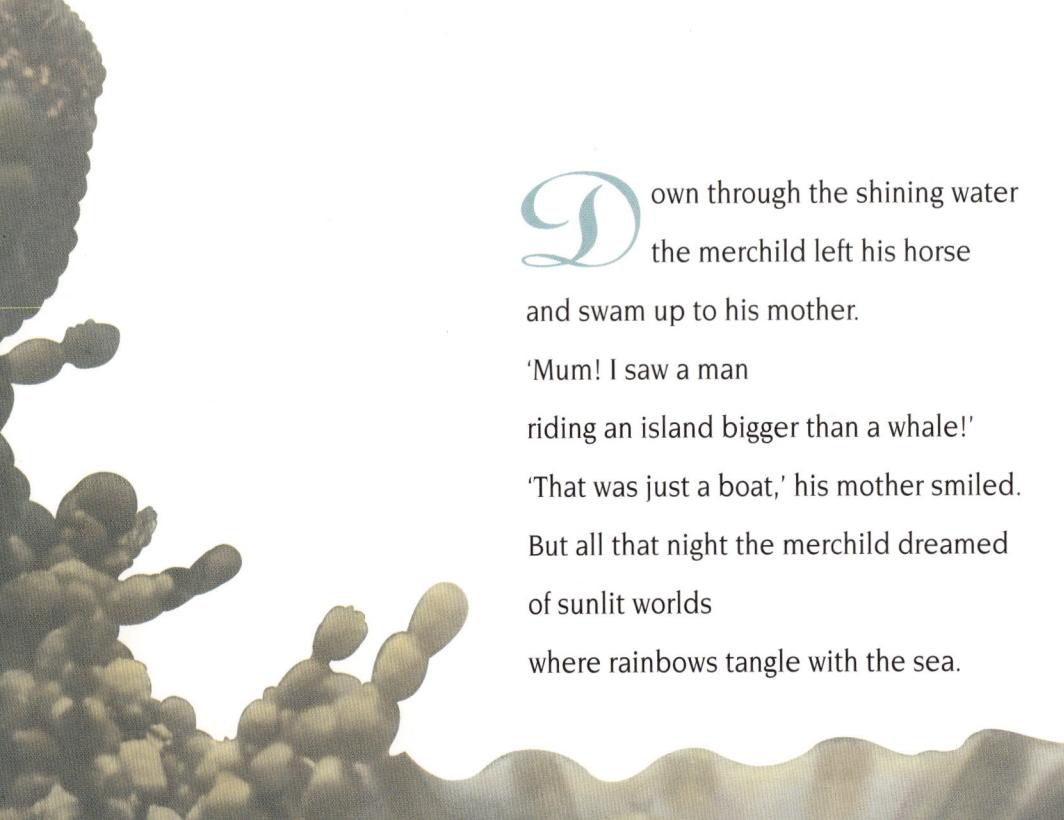

Down through the shining water
the merchild left his horse
and swam up to his mother.
'Mum! I saw a man
riding an island bigger than a whale!'
'That was just a boat,' his mother smiled.
But all that night the merchild dreamed
of sunlit worlds
where rainbows tangle with the sea.

The Lost City

Sitting by the twilight edges of the ocean,
Thirl remembers when the young sun shone upon the Ancient City,
where heroes thought they were stronger than the sea.
For mermaid years are longer than our centuries.

They were proud of their majestic ships in the harbour, the fields of wheat, the power of their beasts and their machines. Then one day their iron failed them and the sea washed through the crumpled streets.

Now only mermaids see the toys rusting in the doorways — the clean bones of buildings where no child will laugh again, the sway of sand that once was drought-burnt paddocks. Only small fish hover where once athletes crouched and the cheers of silence echoed in crumbled stadiums.

Thirl remembers the heroines at their looms and heroes singing. But there are no tears under the sea for Thirl to cry for them.

Bubble

I thought she might be crying, so I swam to her to see.
*'Bubble!' she said, 'bubble!'*
'Are you hungry? Are you sleepy?'
'Bubble!' she said, 'bubble!'

What does 'bubble' mean? I wondered.

But she only waved her tiny fist. 'Bubble!'

she said, 'bubble!'

So I lifted her and swam with her up into the sunlight.

(You need air for babies' voices. Even songs are different in the deep.)

She opened her small mouth and ... giggled.

And as the bubbles floated to the surface

there was laughter all around.

Neptune's Son

*He is a prince sleeping by his kingdom.
You must tread softly if you want to see him.
Creep down the sandhills.
Shh! Try not to make a noise ...
Maybe you'll see him if you're still.*

Yes, he's there,
below the hot white ribbon of the beach,
lying among the treasures of his parents' kingdom;
the seagull prints, and shells, and driftwood from a hundred far off storms,
with small waves nibbling at his scales.

The sea sniffs at his tail, retreats and sniffs again, then pounces at him
cat-like, wanting to play.
The seabirds laugh above the sun-bright spray
till stars' bright circles eddy through the waves.

Later he'll wake
and swim back to the sea
and then play catch with falling stars.

Muses of the Sea

It's hard to keep a harp tuned in sea water;

the salt gets into everything.

You swim off for half an hour and get back to find

the fish have nibbled at the strings.

Or you've just managed to tune C sharp when behind you a whale

groans out B flat

and you've got to start again.

But when the music flows

it comes from everywhere.

A magic of the tides and moon and earth;

and every wave carries

just a little back to shore.

Mermaid's Hair

They said it was only seaweed when I brought it home. Seaweed the colour of old sunlight spilled upon the decks of long forgotten ships.

I found it floating in a rock pool, fine as moonbeams, tangled around a knot of sand and tiny crab claws.

(*I could hear her laugh and protest as she combed it out.*)

When I hung it on the windowsill, I found it never dried but stayed damp with the scent of salt and sea, the last soft echo of the sea-child's call.

Somewhere on another beach, a girl picks up a weed, not realising that it's mermaid's hair.

The Sound of Shells

'Guess what you hear when you listen to a shell?' Lianna whispered.

'Tell me!' Thorda answered. 'I don't know!'

Lianna held the shell up to his ear.

'It's laughter!' Thorda whispered. 'Human laughter!'

Lianna's eyes grew wide. 'It's children playing on the beach!
It's the sound of cars beyond the dunes.
It's kids running at cricket balls.
Dogs barking at the sand.
It's all the echoes of the land.'

Lianna took the shell again and threw it in the sea.

'Why did you do that?' cried Thorda, watching where it splashed.

Lianna smiled. 'One day that shell will float ashore,' she said.
'Maybe a human child will find it.
Maybe they'll hear us.'

Shopping List for a Merbaby

Shells, two dozen bright ones — he only likes to play with coloured shells,

so don't bother collecting dull ones;

at least eight iridescent fish;

seaweed, soft, for napping on — make sure it's not the coarse stuff,

because it makes him itch;

and don't forget the pearl!

You'll get it from the octopus down past the giant clam shell;
who's kept a big one specially,
the sort you can play ball with when you're small
or skittles with the polyps at full moon,
then underwater basketball when he's taller
throwing it in nets of waterweed.
And maybe when he's older
— if he hasn't forgotten it by then, racing off to play tag with passing squid —
he'll roll it down the golden path across the water
till it bounces against the moon.

Swim with Me

*Swim with me softly
through seas thick with foam;
I am a mermaid,
and this is my home ...*

I know where the dolphins play,

twist and curl and laugh in spray.

Swim with me ... this way, this way ...

We'll watch pale seahorses gallop after sweet fish in the bay.

Swim with me ... this way, this way ...

I know where the fishes sleep,

where broken ships their treasure keep,

where hot tides burrow through the winter of the deep

in the green water.

Swim past broken breakers crashing to the land,

swim the moon's bright pathway like a beach of golden sand.

Trust me! Trust me!

Swim beside me as I go ...

I will show you all I know.

Special thanks to

Teighan Busch
Cameron Busch
Jordan Davidson
Karla Marée Dixon
Peter Elfes
John Elfes
Saskia Herbert
Georgia Jeffrey
Jane Coe
Matthew Levitt
Christina Matejcek
Lisa McDonald
Harry Newman
Serena Rojas
Combined Visual Advertising

Hair and make-up
Amber Jeffrey

Stylist
Bernard Rosa, Janine Fuller

Image manipulation
Bernard Rosa, Karoly Szasz

Photography and hand colouring
Bernard Rosa